Mel Bay's

# FUN WITH THE OBOE

by William T. Robinson, III

Illustrations by Donald Howard

1 2 3 4 5 6 7 8 9 0

© 2002 BY MEL BAY PUBLICATIONS, INC., PACIFIC, MO 63069.

*Visit us on the Web at www.melbay.com — E-mail us at email@melbay.com*

# Table of Contents

Parts of the Oboe Reed ............3

Instructions for preparing the reed ............4

Reed Too Open ............6

Reed Too Closed ............6

Drying Out Process ............7

Handmade and Commericial Reeds Can Be Too Open ............7

Adeste Fideles ............10

Alouette ............10

Amazing Grace ............11

America ............11

America the Beautiful ............12

Angels We Have Heard on High ............12

Au Clair de la Lune ............13

Aura Lee ............13

Away in a Manager ............14

Bingo ............14

Chester ............15

Cockles and Mussels ............15

Coventry Carol ............16

Danny Boy ............16

Deep River ............17

Dona Nobis Pacem ............17

The Donkey Song ............18

Down in the Valley ............18

The Drunken Sailor ............19

Fairest Lord Jesus ............19

Faith of Our Fathers ............20

Finlandia ............21

Frére Jacques ............21

Greensleeves ............22

Good King Wenceslas ............22

Hark! The Herald Angels Sing ............23

Home on the Range ............23

Hot Cross Buns ............24

I Would Be True ............24

It Came Upon the Midnight Clear ............25

Jingle Bells ............26

Jolly Old Saint Nicholas ............26

Joy to the World ............27

Kum Ba Ya ............27

Largo from The New World Symphony ............27

Lightly Row ............28

The Little Birch ............28

Little Brown Jug ............29

Loch Lomond ............29

London Bridge ............29

Long, Long Ago ............30

Merrily We Roll Along ............30

The Minstrel Boy ............31

My Lord What a Mornin' ............31

O Come, O Come Emmanuel ............31

O God, Our Help in Ages Past ............32

O Music ............32

Ode to Joy ............32

Old Ark's a-Movin' ............33

Old McDonald ............33

On Springfield Mountain ............33

Onward Christian Soldiers ............34

Polly Wolly ............34

Pomp and Circumstance ............35

Red River Valley ............35

Rejoice and Be Merry ............36

Rock of Ages ............36

Row, Row, Row Your Boat ............37

Shenandoah ............37

Shoo Fly ............38

Simple Gifts ............38

Siyahamba ............39

Skip to My Lou ............39

Swanee River ............40

This Old Man ............40

Tom Dooley ............41

The Victor ............41

We Wish You a Merry Christmas ............42

When the Saints Go Marching In ............42

Yankee Doodle ............43

Yankee Doodle Boy ............43

Fingering Chart ............45

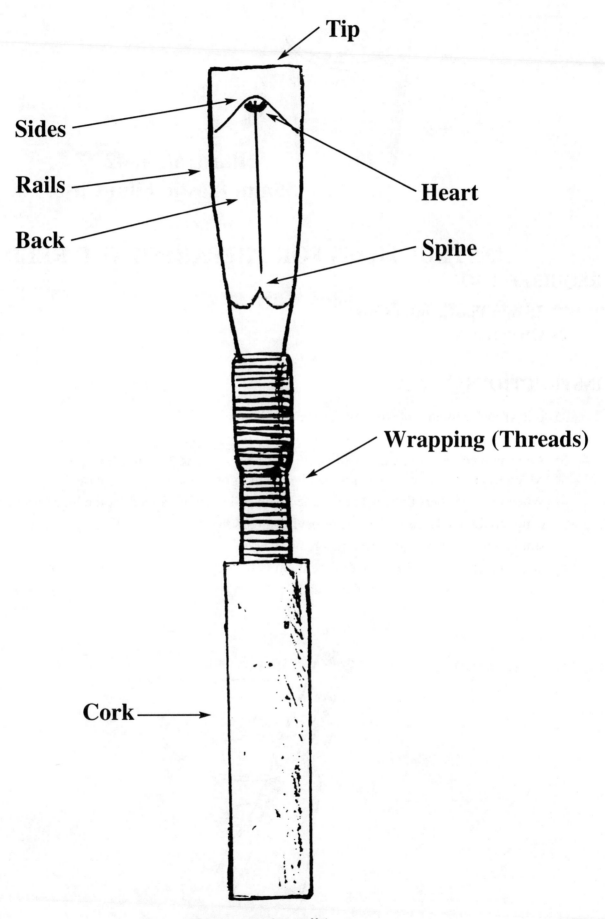

**Illustration #1**
**Parts of the Oboe Reed**

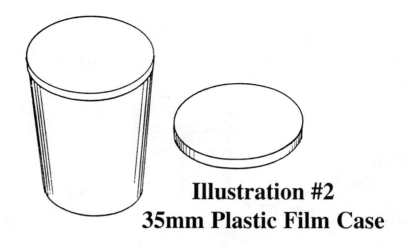

**Illustration #2**
**35mm Plastic Film Case**

# INSTRUCTIONS FOR PREPARING THE REED

**REQUIRED TOOLS:**

1) **35 mm Plastic Film Case**
2) **Oboe Reeds**

## INSTRUCTIONS

1) It is virtually impossible to play the oboe without a properly operating reed.
2) To prepare the reed it is absolutely essential to use a cup of water.
3) Any small container of water will work; however, a plastic 35-mm film case is an excellent cup which has a leak proof top and is small enough to fit inside your oboe case.
4) When one considers the amount of time involved in making a reed, or the high cost of buying commericial reeds, and the value of having a reed that responds well, using a 35 mm film cup or similar container is a good idea that really works.
5) Take one or two oboe reeds and place them in the cup of water, up to the thread on the reed.
6) Avoid letting the water cover the threads.

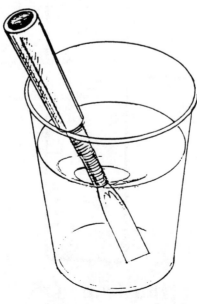

**Illustration #3**

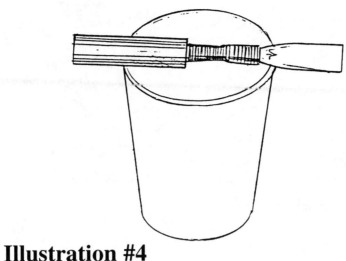

**Illustration #4**

7) Take the reeds out of the water and place them on top of the cup until it is time to play.

8) If the reed is out of the water for a long time before it is played, it will be necessary to place it back in the water.

9) **Remember**, the reed must be moist.

10) If the reeds soak too long, they will become brittle and will not respond well.

11) If they do not soak long enough, they will crack under pressure from the lips or fingers.

**Illustration #5**

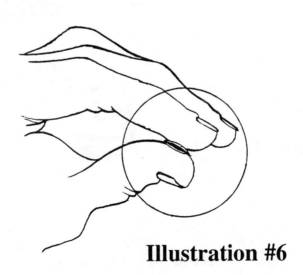

**Illustration #6**

10) Before trying to make the reed crow (the sound one gets on a double reed when blowing the reed without putting it in the oboe well), check the reed aperture (tip opening).

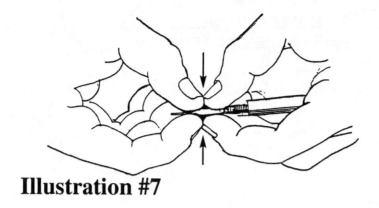

**Illustration #7**

## Reed Too Open

11) If the reed is open too wide, hold the tip with the thumb and first finger of the L.H. and the back of the reed with the thumb and first finger of the R.H.

12) Squeeze gently on the top and bottom of the reed until an oval shape is achieved.

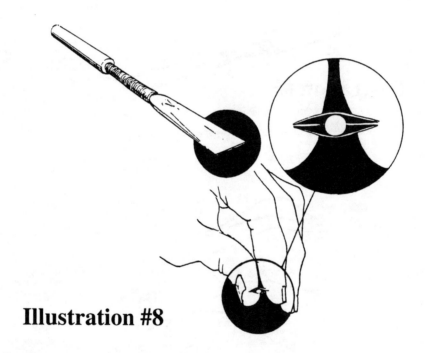

**Illustration #8**

## Reed Too Closed

13) If the reed is closed too much, hold it in one hand by the cork.

14) Take the first finger and thumb of the other hand and gently squeeze the blades on the sides to open the tip to an oval shape.

15) This procedure may have to be repeated several times.

16) **REMEMBER TO KEEP THE REED MOIST.**

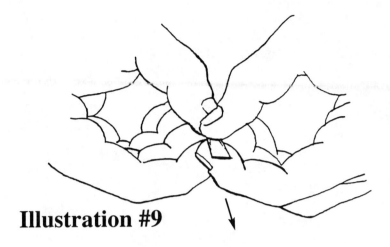

**Illustration #9**

## Drying-Out-Process

17) Each time you wet the reed, take it through the drying-out-process.

18) This process removes excess water from the blades.

19) Pulling the reed gently through the thumb and first finger accomplishes the drying-out-process.

20) Repeat this process until the opening is correct.

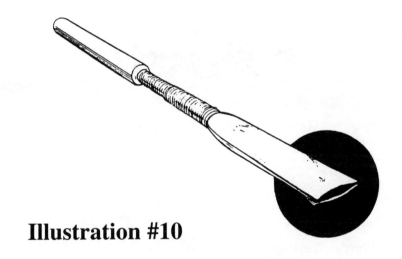

**Illustration #10**

## REED TOO OPEN ON THE SIDES WHEN DRY

21) Many times reeds will open too wide on the sides when they are dry.

22) If the reeds are soaked in water, (not saliva) for about three minutes, the sides will close.

# Songs

# ADESTE FIDELES

Reading

# ALOUETTE

French Folk Song

# AMAZING GRACE

American Melody

# AMERICA

Smith

11

# AMERICA THE BEAUTIFUL

Ward

Moderato

# ANGELS WE HAVE HEARD ON HIGH

French Carol

Moderato

# AU CLAIR DE LA LUNE

French Folk Song

# AURA LEE

Folk Song

# AWAY IN A MANGER

Murry

Legato

# BINGO

Folk Song

Moderato

# CHESTER

Billings

Moderato

# COCKLES AND MUSSELS

Irish Folk Song

Slowly

# COVENTRY CAROL

Old English Carol

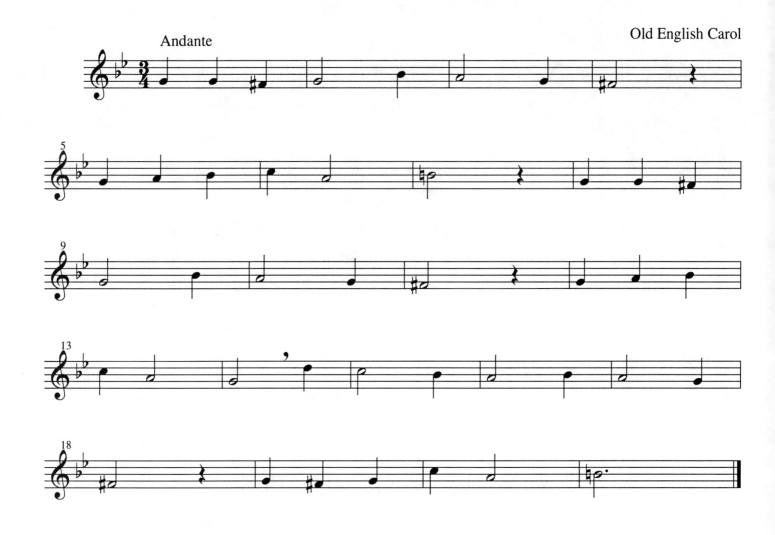

# DANNY BOY

Irish Folk Song

16

# DEEP RIVER

Negro Spiritual

poco a poco rit.

# DONA NOBIS PACEM

Traditional

# THE DONKEY SONG

American Folk Song

Moderato

# DOWN IN THE VALLEY

KENTUCKY FOLK SONG

Andante

# THE DRUNKEN SAILOR

Sea Chanty

# FAIREST LORD JESUS

Hymn

# FAITH OF OUR FATHERS

Hemy

Moderato

# FINLANDIA

Jean Sibelius

Slowly

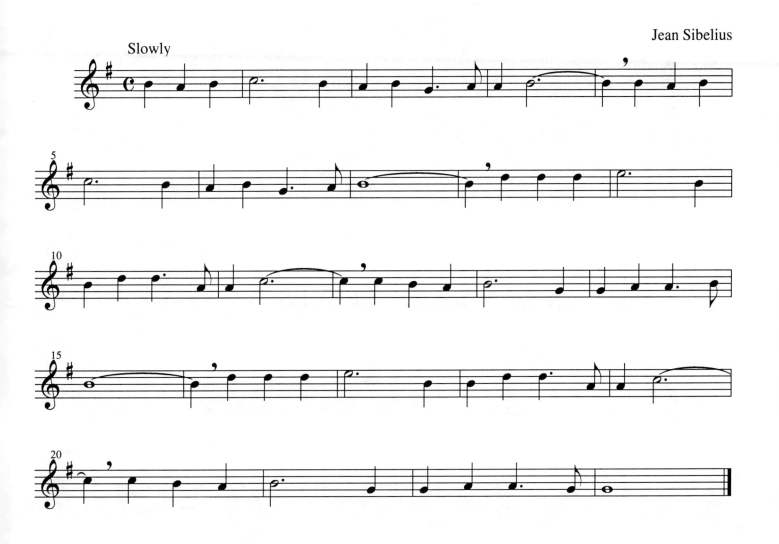

# FRÉRE JACQUES

French Folk Song

Lively

# GOOD KING WENCESLAS

Traditional Carol

Lively

# GREENSLEEVES

Old English Folk Song

Slowly

# HARK! THE HERALD ANGELS SING

Mendelssohn

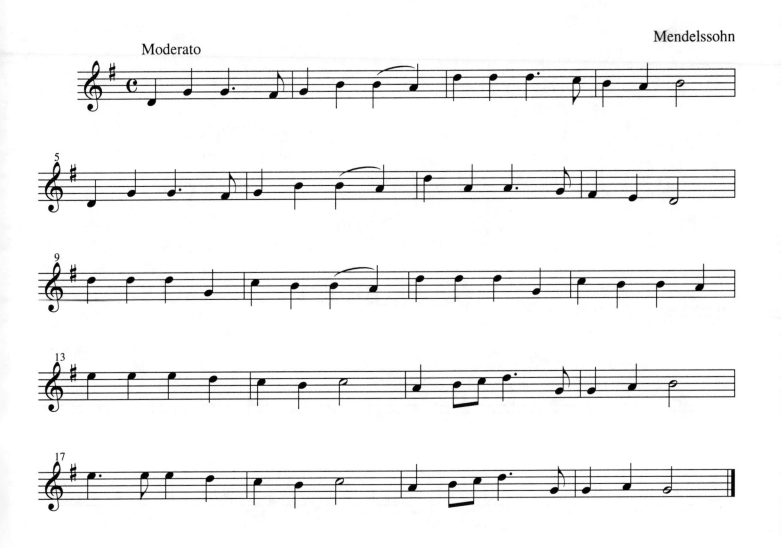

# HOME ON THE RANGE

Cowboy Song

# HOT CROSS BUNS

English Folk Song

# I WOULD BE TRUE

Joseph Yates

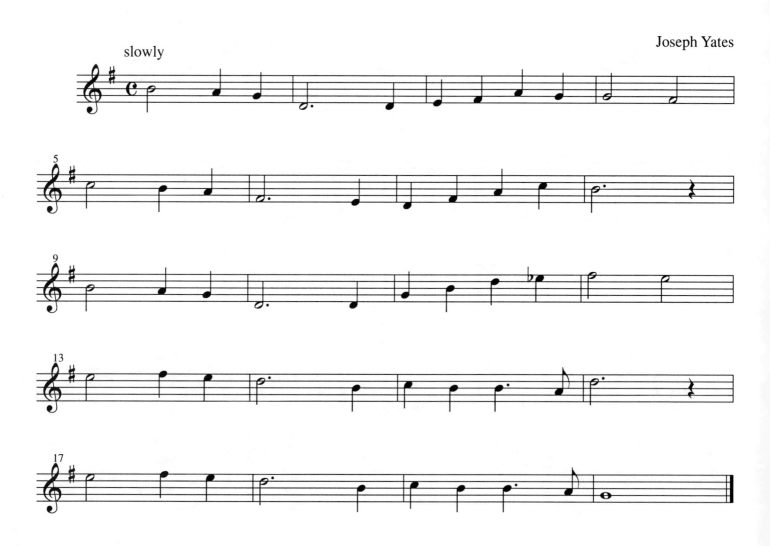

# IT CAME UPON THE MIDNIGHT CLEAR

Willis

Smoothly

# JINGLE BELLS

Traditional Carol

Lightly

# JOLLY OLD SAINT NICHOLAS

Traditional Carol

Lively

# JOY TO THE WORLD

George F. Handel

# KUM BA YA

African Folk Song

# *LARGO* FROM THE NEW WORLD SYMPHONY

DVORAK

# LIGHTLY ROW

Folk Song

# THE LITTLE BIRCH

Russian Folk Song

# LITTLE BROWN JUG

Folk Song

Lively

# LOCH LOMOND

Moderately

Scotch Folk Song

# LONDON BRIDGE

Folk song

Moderato

# LONG, LONG AGO

Folk Song

Moderato

# MERRILY WE ROLL ALONG

Folk Song

Gaily

# THE MINSTREL BOY

Irish Folk Song

Moderato

# MY LORD WHAT A MORNIN'

Negro Spiritual

Adagio

# O COME, O COME EMMANUEL

Plainsong

Freely

# O GOD, OUR HELP IN AGES PAST

Watts

Majestically

# O MUSIC

Lowell Mason

With Spirit

# ODE TO JOY

Beethoven

Moderato

# OLD ARK'S A-MOVIN'

Traditional

# OLD MCDONALD

Folk Song

# ON SPRINGFIELD MOUNTAIN

Folk Song

# ONWARD CHRISTIAN SOLDIERS

Sullivan

# POLLY WOLLY

Folk Song

# POMP AND CIRCUMSTANCE

Elgar

Grand March

# RED RIVER VALLEY

Cowboy Song

Slowly

# REJOICE AND BE MERRY

German Folk Song

Lively

# ROCK OF AGES

Thomas Hasting

Moderato

# ROW, ROW, ROW YOUR BOAT

Folk Song

Merrily

# SHENANDOAH

Folk Song

Slowly

# SHOO FLY

Folk Song

# SIMPLE GIFTS

Shaker Melody

# SIYAHAMBA

Zula Folk Song

# SKIP TO MY LOU

Mountain Dance

# SWANEE RIVER

Foster

With Spirit

# THIS OLD MAN

Folk Song

Lively

40

# TOM DOOLEY

Folk Song

# THE VICTOR

L. Elber

# WE WISH YOU A MERRY CHRISTMAS

English Folk Song

Lively

# WHEN THE SAINTS GO MARCHING IN

Traditional

With Spirit

# YANKEE DOODLE

American Folk Song

Lively

# YANKEE DOODLE BOY

Cohan

With Spirit

# Fingering Chart

# CHROMATIC FINGERING CHART FOR
# THE BEGINNING OBOIST

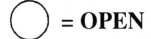 = OPEN        = CLOSE

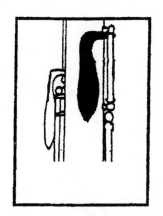

**FIRST OCTAVE KEY**
located on the back of the oboe,
played with the left hand thumb

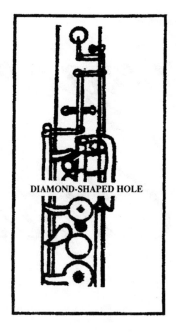

DIAMOND-SHAPED HOLE

**HALF HOLE**
Roll the first finger
of the left hand
halfway off of the
finger plate to
expose the
diamond shaped
hole.

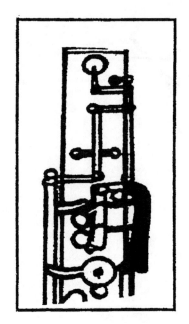

**SECOND OCTAVE KEY**
located on the upper joint,
played with the side of the left hand
first finger

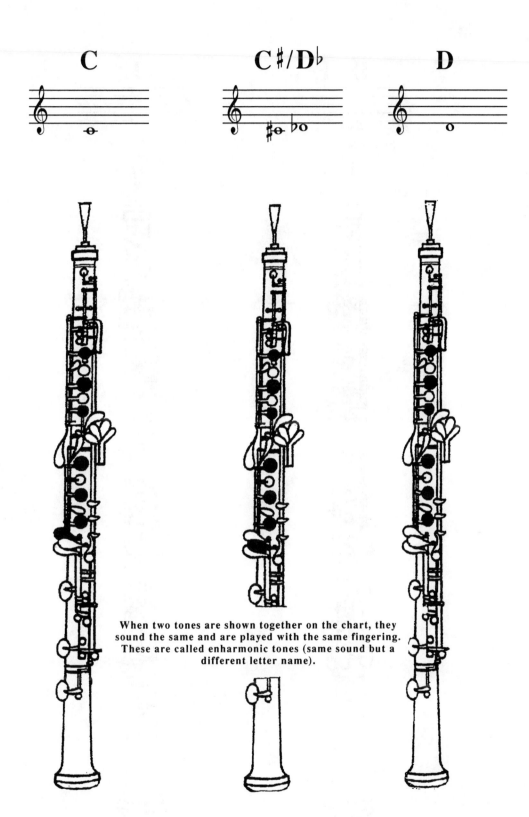

When two tones are shown together on the chart, they sound the same and are played with the same fingering. These are called enharmonic tones (same sound but a different letter name).

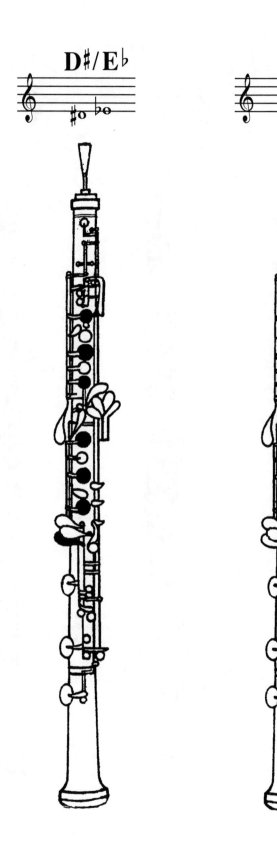

# REGULAR F

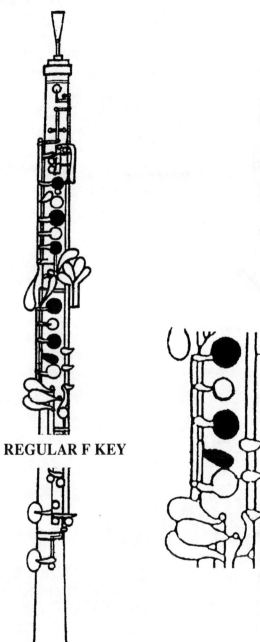

**REGULAR F KEY**

# FORKED F

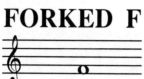

# F#/G♭

The forked F should be used when F comes
before or after D, D#/E♭, C#/D♭.

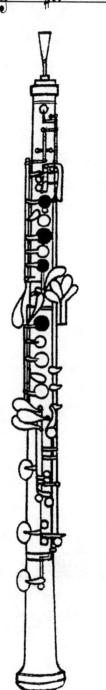

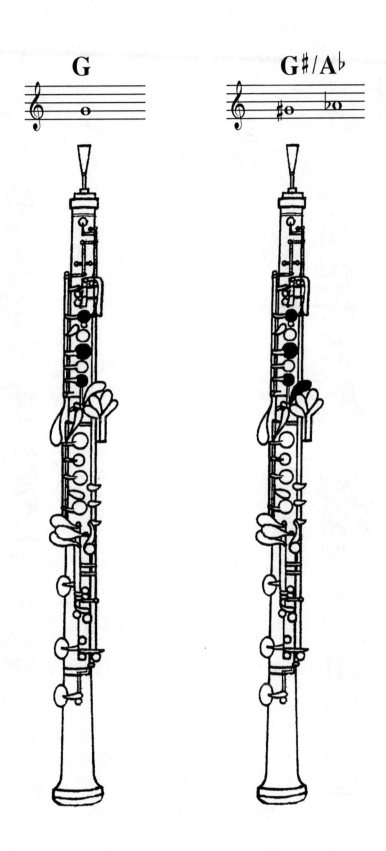

**A**

**A♯/ B♭**

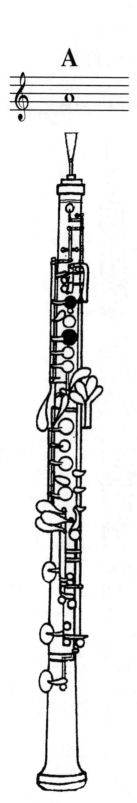

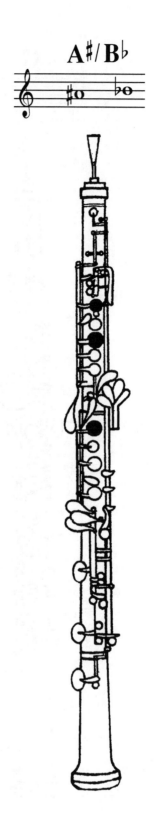

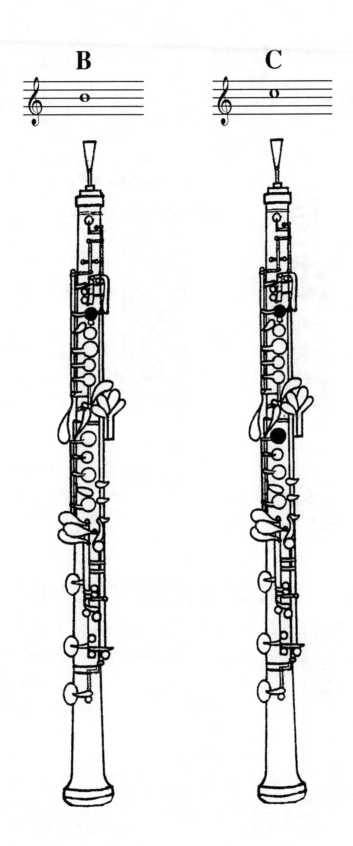

# C♯/D♭

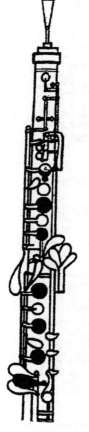

**Play C♯/D♭, D, D♯/E♭
with the half hole**

**DIAMOND SHAPED HOLE**

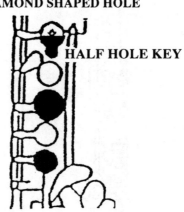

**HALF HOLE KEY**

**Roll the first finger of the left hand halfway off of the finger plate to expose
the diamond shaped hole when you play C♯/D♭, D, D♯/E♭.**

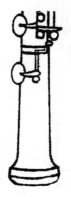

**D**

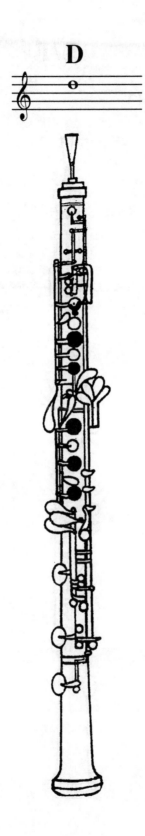

# D♯/E♭

# E

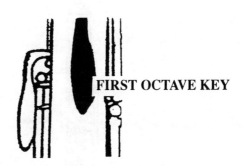

**FIRST OCTAVE KEY**

**Play E, regular F, forked F, F♯/G♭, G, G♯/A♭ with the first octave key on the back of the oboe.**

# REGULAR F

# FORKED F

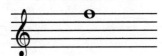

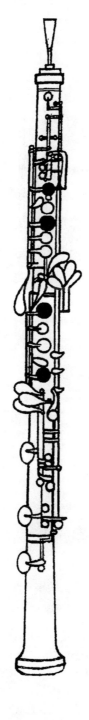

Forked F should be used when F
comes before or after C♯/D♭, D,
D♯/E♭.

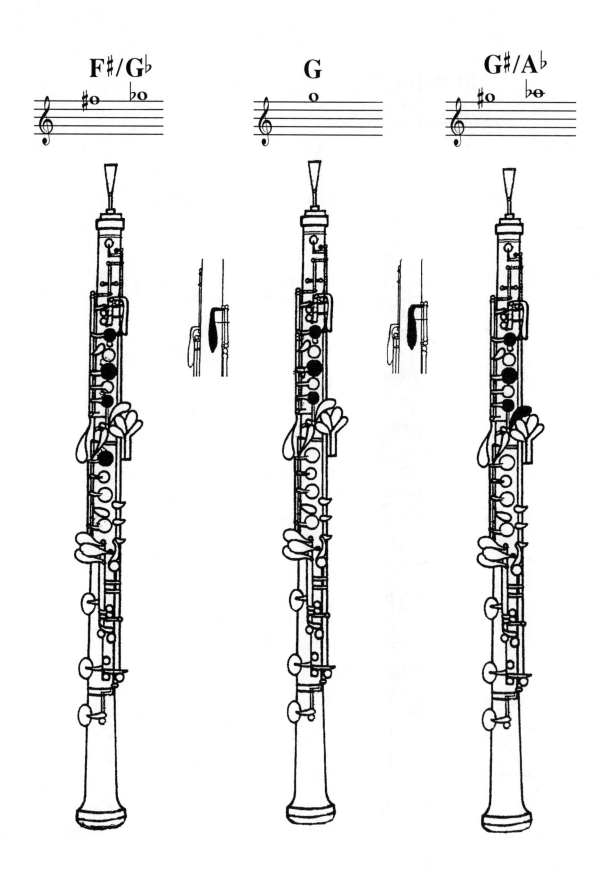

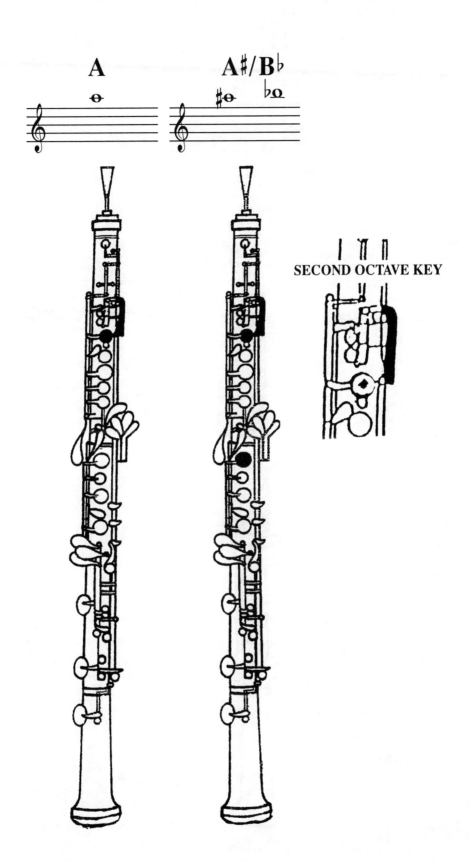

SECOND OCTAVE KEY

**B**

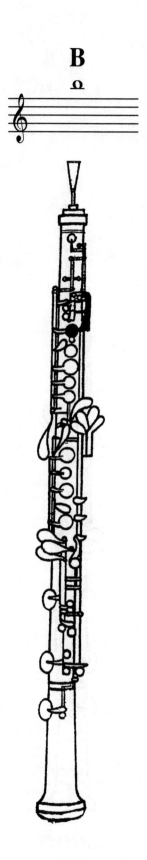

# C

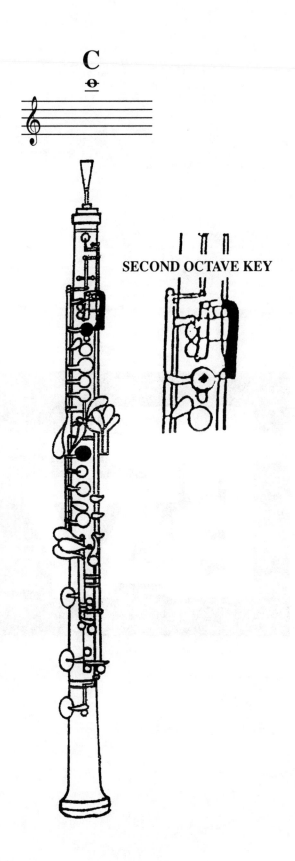

**SECOND OCTAVE KEY**